Terrain

JEAN HARRISON

CinnamonPress
INDEPENDENT INNOVATIVE INTERNATIONAL

Published by Cinnamon Press
Meirion House, Glan yr afon, Tanygrisiau
Blaenau Ffestiniog, Gwynedd, LL41 3SU
www.cinnamonpress.com

ISBN: 978-1-907090-69-1

British Library Cataloguing in Publication Data. A CIP record for this book can be obtained from the British Library.

Designed and typeset in Palatino by Cinnamon Press
Cover from original artwork 'Aerial of Mountain Road by Rebekah Burgess © Agency: dreamstime.com
Cover design by Jan Fortune

Printed in Poland

Cinnamon Press is represented in the UK by Inpress Ltd www.inpressbooks.co.uk and in Wales by the Welsh Books Council www.cllc.org.uk

Thanks

Thanks are due to a large number of people who have given advice and encouragement, especially Jan Fortune who believed in my writing, also Carole Bromley, Carole Coates, Jane Routh, Irene Rawnsley and Sue Vickerman. And most of all, of course, Barbara Bowman. There is also a deposit of earlier teaching from The Poetry Business (the Poetry School invaluable) and Meg Peacocke that still surfaces, providing guidance and useful questions.

Acknowledgements

Poems in this collection have previously appeared in *Smiths Knoll, The North, Brittle Star, Envoi* and *Interpreter's House.*

Contents

Disturbances:

Elegy:

for Barbara

Disturbances

Disturbances

1. Invigilating

Sitting and watching,
walking around and watching
in a space where nothing much

appears to be happening –
you're like the Ancient Roman 'vigil',
sentinel, nightwatchman – there to notice

an over-large bag, a foot over a line,
a nose breathing out droplets
onto a fragile surface.

If needed, *call a member of staff – don't attempt*
to operate the disabled hoist. The request
could be a diversionary tactic.

Sometimes
when the room's empty,
silent inside closed shutters,

the watching goes up in the world
as in a chapel where someone waits
on the eve of a saint's day –

though pigments, pencil, canvas, paper
in wooden frames fastened to stone walls
shouldn't, logically, cause any disturbance.

2. Taking over

I take the badge, find how to clip it on,
ask my predecessor
to show me yet again where
to press the walkie-talkie, remind her
to take her bag, excuse myself for thinking
she might forget, *I left my coat in the car*
because of my memory. She says,
Mine's in the cloakroom, goes.

And then the quiet, the lowered voices,
the company of colour bursting off plain walls.

3. Terrain

David Jones
Pencil and watercolour on paper

His pencil's run up a ridge of volcanic rock,
probed hollows, outlined an isolated hill,
indicated boulders lodged in a gorge.

Flicks, delicate and precise
as the course of a sniper's bullet, show
where stone breaks softer edges.

He's given full details of the foreground valley
taken time over stone walls, ash trees,
a barn where a farmer might be about.

He inspects this countryside
from a commanding position
as a hunter might, or a surveyor

a draughtsman with a mind dyed
by legend and history, an eye
trained on a landscape

that's probably Wales, maybe the Borders,
seeing it still as terrain, though it's peaceful now
under moving cloud shadows.

4. Chair

Sometimes I wait an age
for a viewer to send waves
rippling across the room
as he or she takes care
not to look this way,
but moves sideways, soundlessly
facing the jewelled wall while I,
here to stay awake and keep watch,
don't look up –
let her (or him) have peace
to love in. My role to be the chair
a cat curls on, half-asleep,
still sensitive to body-heat, alert
the moment a mouse scratches.

5. From the artist's window 1916

Robert Bevan
Oil on canvas

Dull

The art group has decided this picture shows nothing
except that the artist looked down from a high window
onto a North London street on a morning in 1916
and recorded what he saw:
                                        a three-storey stuccoed terrace,
two old men, one bent on a stick, the other tiny and hunched;
a woman with a small child, a maid lifting a parcel from a cart;
a hansom - the driver with stiff shoulders, white hair visible
on the nape of his neck; two older women on their way
to shops perhaps or a committee. No-one hurrying.

The whole scene in subdued colour and correct perspective
except for one tree – most probably a cypress, probably also
genuinely there, dull blue-green foliage flattened,
streaked with black, angled sideways and up
with harsh edges, the way war-artists on the Somme
depicted guns, as if for a moment he was distracted
from meticulous observation of civilians
left at home, keeping things going.

6. Flying over, orange and purple

Wilhelmina Barns-Graham
Oil on canvas

I'm stuck in front of this one
though I wouldn't want it on my wall.

It's not its fault
that blue
dominating the foreground
is the colour of my mother's dress –
there's no figure there bending, holding out her arms,
saying, *Bury your head here.*

These shapes and colours are pulled away
from real life, though one shape
seems to be in the air definitely flying,
others are underneath.

That lurid red could be sky, the blue in front
a strip of sea which someone I'm not admitting to
and who isn't in the picture
decides must be the Channel, the flare not sunrise.

There's no-one either, lying on that winged shape
flat on their stomach in tilted purple darkness
in a plane that's only hinted at
with shells in the lockers

looking down over grey and deep blue,
sleeping houses perhaps
fields stripped white by searchlights
a yard where bombs will soon fall.

The cellar, where a child's running to hide,
could be blown open.

I sat there listening to guns.

This picture needs a place to itself,
a back room where I wouldn't often go.

7. A boy in a purple tee-shirt

which makes him stand out
in a roomful of the soberly dressed
middle aged, that and the still soft
contours of his face –

lurches toward the end wall.
tilts his head, comes close, considers
the painting sideways a long time,
wanders on, slowly in heavy trainers.

A thin woman (perhaps his mother)
catches up and stands beside him,
murmurs something authoritative.
He listens, head turned away, seems

not to find a focus. Do his mates
discuss this kind of thing?
It's probably not cool, or whatever
the latest word is.

The artist died something like
fifteen years before he was born.
Maybe wordless judgements are forming.
I don't think he's bored –

after his eyes have gone vague and
he seems almost ready to chew his fingers,
he suddenly lumbers off towards
a view of houses under heavy cloud.

8. Feet

I watch feet,
the distance they keep from walls,

and less officially, the quiet patterns
boots and shoes trace out across the floor:

a two-footed 180° right spin on leather soles,
just inside the doorway

a long stand, followed by three steps back – almost everyone
takes the same number –

a religious walk – heavy sandals
pacing under hands clasped over the stomach

a sideways prowl of size nines
a slow rise onto the toes and down

a dart forward,
then back, quick, quick, slow.

And once, in the centre of the floor, a stationary circle
toes turned inwards

9. Cumberland

Sheila Fell
Oil on canvas

Her birth date's not far off mine.

This woman from a bleak northern village
who'd always wanted to paint –
there's her photo in the catalogue
and her story – she wasn't afraid to shock –
and me, with my held-in southern conventional way,
if we'd met before she fell downstairs
is there any hope we'd have got on?

Her work's still here

and now a shape,
bent over the handlebars of a
heavy bicycle towing a wooden trailer
melts into a man in North-west Kent
who rode so slowly it was a miracle
the machine stayed upright.

Smudged figures in empty streets,
louring cloud, the hold of snow,
dark clefts in assertive hills –

a dream-world she created in London
holding onto a county
whose name was being swept off the map

In Yorkshire today I imagine
I can taste *Coe's Golden Drop* –
bags of sweet juice ripened against yellow brick,
can still walk a dank path curving down
between walls of knapped flint,
though I know
the garden's under bungalows now.

10. What?

She seems to know
something most of us don't

but what?

The hidden side of Skiddaw
that faces north? An intenser green
than the one which comes sometimes
in early summer in diffused light
under storm cloud? How timeless men look
doing heavy fieldwork at sunset, the earth
glowing as if from internal fire?

I can work this much out.

11. Hounds

The catalogue's kept tied to one leg
of the bench in the middle room.

Most of the time it lies doggo
while people walk past. Later

some come back, looking thoughtful.
They tug the string, struggle

to flatten out the pages – it's kept
on a very tight lead – turn them over

till suddenly
eyes focus, a body leans, a hand rises

brushes a cheek, rests there,
then drops, holds the looking still –

two women like pointers, one seated,
the other gazing over her friend's shoulder –

an old man who twists his long legs sideways,
curves his chest forward over the thighs

profile first hovering, then closing in on the text
as if scenting a hare. Silence

rises around them like morning mist.

12. Sunsets

In her world
people never do well,

always blurred or small, at one side
picking potatoes or loading a cart,

or alone, cycling into wind.
Those forms smudged against a sunset

are probably human. Round them
the earth's melting back into lava.

I stand back.
She must have lived with these fears.

Look at this group of walkers on a beach,
how waves curve down over them like tsunamis

I know only from TV, observing tiny figures
in boats, at windows, swept off bridges.

Aid workers struggle in yellow jackets,
water rushes up the street, wind flattens the palms.

Reporters pick out the drama
flailing legs, tears, bodies.

The sun's taking its revenge,
preparing to shrivel the earth, they say

It's all our fault they say, showing pictures
from the other side of the world

that come up on a screen
framed by curtains and a softly painted wall.

Next morning, no greenfinches in the garden.
There haven't been any for ages.

13. Sean Scully

Wall of light, red summer, Yucatan'
Oil on canvas

Stone wall in full sun in a hot country.
Does it separate fields, enclose a barn
or crumble along with other ruins? No-one knows
who burnt down the palaces.

There's red, the shade of newly hardened blood,
pink like flesh under a burst blister, some ochre
and black – two charred blocks
in opposite corners.

In the museum a king
offers a man's heart to the sun; his queen
pulls cactus through a hole in her tongue.
A glyph explains, *She shed her blood.*

This seems a rough, ordinary wall, worked
from a sketch, photo, or memory
the painter held by the way
varying sizes of oblong and square
laid to fit, horizontal or vertical
with rounded corners and wavy edges,

will shimmer at midday
composed of light, blasted
from the sun where all earth's colours are born.

Did his mind enter that savagery and work inside it,
his arms remember heat, how at the end of that afternoon
the skin inside his shirt was red and peeled next day?

14. Skin

Sometimes when I sit on my own, my skin
becomes porous to greens, blacks, pinks, reds that flame off
the walls.
I feel light as a beachball on water, a floating eye,

though I'm still disturbed by *tap-tap* on wooden stairs
on the landing, then quiet
and I follow a curator

as she unlocks that door marked 'Private'
into a room with unbroken walls all round.
How do they light it? It's too low in the house for a skylight.

Here, white painted windows boarded up
create an enclosure like the monastery in Florence
where each cell has one wall filled

by an Angelico nativity, crucifixion or resurrection,
and as a monk sleeps, reads, prays, contemplates,
a vision streams out and dyes his life.

15. Munich Mirrors

Sean Scully
Oil on canvas

five rectangles
on a white wall
narrow columns
striped horizontally –
campaign ribbons
or football scarves?
each one different
no illusion of depth

striped scarves
with a lot of red in them
labelled *Munich?*
what should I think?
called *Mirrors?*
flat surfaces
reflecting here
something else perhaps

1958 and
seven dead men
whose faces
I didn't know
even then –
nothing to do with
coloured boxes
not meant to imply

white space like snow

blank places on a pitch

those empty

days of grief?

no words
only stripes
that lie across –
six foot lengths – ?
I gaze
where a title
started up the play
of like and unlike.

16. For love (Robert Creeley)
from 'First Series, Some Poets'

R B Kitaj
Six colour screenprint on paper

He paints the head in pastels

photographs the painting

transfers the image to silk and prints.

Looks a long time.

Puts it away.

Perhaps re-reads Creeley, notes
short lines, subdued, powerful rhythms,

draws four rulers, labels each one
inches and eighths,

lays them down as a frame

from which the poet breaks free.

So it's OK to be slow?

Draft after draft, layer upon layer

17. Stack

Prunella Clough
Oil on canvas

Rough oblong on its narrow end,
off-centre in a huge canvas, a pile
of orange and blue uneven stripes and shadows,
no rhythm of same size, same shape,

perhaps as a notice suggests,
a heap of small plastic plates.
I see it first as a tower-block,
rows of lit windows against greys

that make them lonely. Her *urbscape*
ferments in her:
sprawl of a broken fence,
sheen of puddles on waste-land.

She places them high on her canvas,
like lock gates in East London
above a canal basin
looked down on by three storeys

of broken windows, a hole
where I entered
the endurance of heavy timber,
the quiet of concrete. I notice now

she pays twists of rusty barbed wire
the loving attention a birder
gives to an eye-stripe,
or a style of perching or probing,

that things she paints
belong to man-made places
which have given up on people
but are still caught by light.

She's investigating
its effects again
filtering through the material and joints
of a stack of variously coloured plastic plates.

18. Feet and inches

The head's clear from a distance
in some kind of broken frame and also
four faint white lines, two horizontal,
two vertical. I walk across. They're rows of
squiggles – oh – letters I turn my head
as needed. They all say, *Feet and inches.*
each row parallel to a ruler. They're
what makes the frame. Reddish brown. Squared up
halo? Does he need to point out these are tools
for measuring? I've done plenty of that.
Drew triangles at school. Since then
planning a new dress, I've looked at myself,
considered my height/weight ratio.
Yesterday I stood by the cold-frame, gazed
at my neighbour's Leylandii and saw
how tall my plants could grow if that hedge
were only six feet. Kitaj's confusing me,
making pictures spring in my mind with no
apparent relevance to his screenprint.

Arranging a life of forms on a surface
is the bread and butter of painting
So it's the shape of *Feet and inches*
that counts? Or…?
Which side of my brain am
I supposed to use?

The life of words, feeding my mind.

Two viewers arrive. Stop griping, watch them.
Perhaps Robert Creeley wrote poems about
feet and inches? Don't think so but you never
know. Better get back to my chair. I can
go on thinking about this.

19. L S Lowry

Oil on canvas
Gentry

Those iron gates flanked by stone gateposts
don't look as if they'd ever let me in. I'll never
walk that dead straight alley to a white house
with narrow windows. Acres of mown grass
behind the row of poplars that throw such
evenly spaced shadows, may be referred to
as a deer park. I can't imagine its owners
would allow even domesticated
beasts to wander on their perfect sward.
These people would wear imposing hats,
tight breeches or long skirts and underneath
be wooden, almost peg dolls, except their legs
would move. I can imagine them walking,
in a dignified way, never sitting, eating,
tilting their heads, laughing. Democrat
peering through railings, I get this idea –
I'd like to take them swimming. They'd
be able to float, might slowly learn to bend and flex.

20. An elaborate robe – or Portrait of the artist as schliemiel

yiddish – awkward, unlucky fellow

R Kitaj
Oil on canvas

The boy's eleven maybe, stops, stands,
runs to his mother in the next room,
comes back with the canvas bag,
coils down onto the floor and looks up,
smoothes out a square of white paper,
leans forward, places the first mark,
deepens it, sits upright again,
licks the tip of his pencil, returns to rubbing,
bending lower, bowing towards the floor
with white knuckles. His hand lays down
its crayon, hovers – This one? – No, this.

No-one's ever worn such a robe –
so many perky stained-glass rhomboids
spread over gesturing silk
that hides and reveals a man.

From here I can't make out – and it's
none of my business – if the child's seen
the twist of those powerful shoulders.
one arm flung sideways, the other
raised and bent so the back of the hand
brushes the spine in a second of calm
before it'll be flailed back up.

Does he take in the yellow head
thrust onto the left shoulder, facing
impossibly backwards? Bared teeth?
Harsh green omission marks
above no eyes?

He's left a blank above the robe. Perhaps
he's seen through wizards and ogres. He seems
to be focussing on the next colour.

21. Interrogating Kitaj

Don’t you need to fling paint onto canvas

I’m drawing very slowly.

let the blood, adrenalin or whatever other
hormone drives you, let rip
so your darting and sweeping hand
itself becomes a sunset, a vase, an eye?

Drawing

If you take time to think, worry, judge, change
won’t the edges become too sharp, or wobble,
the whole thing plod?

very

Does a cat
ever come close enough to pin down a mouse
without that sprint?

slowly

Are you a chartmaker
plotting oil-bearing rock from echoes
bounced off the sea bed?

I’m getting lost in this. Good.

A child sleepwalking downstairs?

Getting
lost.
Drawing
very
slowly.

22. Keep it dark

(This is the Friday the authorities
had better not hear about, the day
I'm in danger of nodding off. Thursday
I rushed to catch a train to meet a friend,
then late afternoon helped a carer transport
an old person's heavy computer,
shopped, listened to intense talk
about emotional problems,
lay awake in the small hours. Perhaps
should have phoned in but how could they
find someone better at short notice?

I sit, with a book on my lap, hoping
if the worst happens, the volume
will clatter onto the floor. No cords
to pull up blinds that keep falling,
half-time coffee without effect, figures
waver like smoke before my eyes.
At last, thank heavens, a visitor asks
why RB Kitaj hadn't finished
the portrait of Wolfheim and Angela
[a man with a cat that's sitting on air]
and I come awake in his dreamworld
trying to work out why he did it.)

23. Daphne Charlton

Stanley Spencer
Oil on canvas

Off duty, perched on a child-sized stool
for a lecture about your life, I look up at your
more than life-size head
and wonder

what it was like for you being, not
the Hilda he divorced and went on
to the end of his life begging
to re-marry him, nor the Patricia
he married, piled with jewels
but never made love to,

just his third woman, the one
he had to share, the only one
who sewed on his buttons, whom
he painted four times:
                                        in a hat
with one half-hidden red rose;
                                                    nude,
grappling with him on a tiger-skin rug;

with gigantic breasts and folded arms
outfacing the village gossips while he
buries his head in your shoulder. Did you
enjoy being his guardian angel?

At least this time he's shown you serious,
in an olive blouse with well combed auburn hair,
has paid attention to every millimetre
as if he couldn't have enough of flesh –
cheeks, chin, nose, forehead –

Your green eyes look away. Your lips are soft
and open a little towards him. I look up
and take in details of your private life.
You're exposed there, alone on that wall.

24. Pressures

Long, narrow room.
Charcoal, pencil, black paint.
No windows. Solitary
confinement

condemned to watch
sad eyes, sensitive,
down-turned mouths,
faces that fill frames
and float
in isolation –

even a friend with his cat –
the man's deeply furrowed face
half amused, tender, thoughtful
looks down not
at the animal but his own hand.

I'm moved to another room
and still I'm shut in
with Kitaj's fury
against Fascism,
the murder of Elsa Luxembourg,
the plight of refugees,
his dark examining of Wagner's eyes.

What can I say?

My thoughts slip

through the walls to a friend
who struggles to hold on
in a large, remote house, battles
still, now, to be herself, batters
friends, neighbours, carers, giggles
when they can't lift her, wordlessly
rages because something
is undoing her muscles, one by one.

25. It's not always rapture – so

go through my handbag: Purse,
chequebook, supermarket receipts.
Smooth them out, pile them,
refold the bundle, put it back –
not enough here for Inspector Morse
to build up a picture of my habits.
Dust. Crumbs. No comb – .
Battered card for Craven taxis.
Ditto for B and B in Windermere.
Good place. Ages ago. Keep it?
Three black pens – surely the other day
one of them was blue? No note-book, diary.
No watch on my wrist. Time here
in and out of notice. Arrive, settle,
watch people, watch empty room,
stretch legs, go for coffee, return,
watch more people, observe the angles
of spotlights that cast creamy light
on walls and portraits. Layered shadows –
petals. Go on sitting, become familiar
with the motionless faces of strangers.

26. Untitled

Mohammed Ali Tapir
Ink on paper

Seen from the next room –
        lines like falling rain blown sideways
                but sharper, definitely black,

then moving like a thread curtain
        over fragments of the Elgin marbles.
                A few steps closer

the humps are fibrous
        like the underside of soft bark
                or handfuls of coir.

Nearer still it's vanes of a wing-feather
        coming apart, waiting for fingers
                to smooth them together.

My nose almost touching,
        the ink seems to stand up
                as if these were linen threads

just now unwound from a reel
        laid on the paper
                still holding a curl

too stiff for this rippling. More likely
        the artist let the pen lead him
                as if water was pulling down his hand

to make it wander
        the way a drop runs
                and extends down a pane

swerves sideways
        snagged by something
                on the glass

swings back, follows
        the rules of its own fluidity and mass
                and yet is free

and he obeyed as if enticed by birdsong
        not looking for a thrush
                but absorbed in its phrasing.

27. Coir

How many square metres,
hard-wearing, resilient, patterned by texture,
are needed to lie at the foot of this brilliance
and make the rooms feel warm?

It's only the tousled hair of a nut
which grows hanging over a beach
absorbing reflected sunlight –
white sand and green breakers –

relies on the sea to carry it
in a home-grown life-jacket
to take root somewhere else,
use its wrapping as compost

and this fibre, slashed off, combed, twisted,
with all those colours tingling inside it,
damps down sound here
as efficiently as leaf-mould.

28. Love

In the mysterious way of love, he says
describing his habit of copying one particular artist
morning after morning before his own work,

the way some viewers don't follow numbers round the room
but stand in the doorway, wait for an impulse that sends them
the whole length of a diagonal sometimes, to stand and stare,

the way I'm held by this depiction of the head and shoulders
of a lorry driver squared up to fit his cab, at one with his vehicle:
the chunky hands of Lowestoft fishermen

and then by a line a draughtsman took for a flight across paper
following a bird, a duck to judge from the way it faltered, looped
back
perhaps searched fields, hedges, a valley for water and its mate,

the mysterious way of love that sometimes doesn't open – green
towering waves
everyone says have such energy –and it's as if I'm standing at a
distance
in cold wind, thinking how hard the painter was working to keep
warm.

Elegy

Swotting

Saturday afternoon in the library,
every seat taken, we're swotting for finals.

A cuckoo keeps on outside the window,
Come out, make love, you're wasting the sunshine.

We take no notice, boning up on things
that exercise the minds of academics

e.g. did Plato slip once and imagine
the *Being-of-a-Horse* eating grass?

If so, perhaps he wasn't wrong,
just slid over into contemplation -

pure existence galloping – there's
a subject for a wild-life photographer -

track it into its habitat, hide
till it stands still – a lifetime's affair

which could be multi-media - there's scope
for paint music words silent gazing

The examiners aren't interested in guff.
What you need is results. That bird

is a model of self-indulgence. It
doesn't even look after its own egg.

Learning to walk

A small child edges sideways
left foot then right, plants each firmly
clings onto banisters

looks through and down
towards feet slowly climbing steps, stopping
as a door clicks, voices gust out,

goes on testing how you steady a body
against wooden uprights,
looking down the vertical face of a wall.

The sound

reaches you, through a closed window at night, not the roar
of a motor-bike surging over the railway bridge or lads larking in the
        street.
This sound is silent and has come to get you where it knows you are,
muddled under a duvet.

It plants its feet on you like a cat, each one a jab into your soft belly,
knows you've confused its quiet entrance with the watching moon
that's sailed in to show roofs and walls in a new light,
blurring brick and slate, friendly to rats,

the world out there no longer the one you go through in the daytime
with its traffic lights, shop windows, colleagues –
who aren't saying what they think. They're not the only ones.
Every eye shows it. You lie awake and listen to them now.

The wrong side of the tracks

There's that girl again
walking in the wet dark
though she has a room with a fire

but she's restless, knowing
there are things to see, places to go
outside and different – an alley

that leads in the opposite direction
from library, department store, a pond with swans.
It takes her to an embankment and iron fence,

wind blowing through gantries high above.
She thinks of Wuthering Heights,
Catherine calling, *Let me in.*

A rusty bridge inside the nearest arch
leads her above a canal,
footsteps echoing up into grimy brick,

then down to worn grass,
an estate of pebble-dashed houses,
a woman with draggled hair

who runs stops gabbles
I stuck the stamp on upside down –
that wet on her face isn't just rain –

her eyes are white marbles – *They say*
it's an insult to the Queen –
I've posted it.

Surely someone must know her,
could take her home, wrap her in a towel, rub her hair?
No-one comes running.

Tapping

Rain on the skylight, a small fingernail
that taps then stops
as if a child has been told to get out from under everyone's feet,

stands now cramped by a navy gabardine, gazes at the garden,
fingers up and down on the latch of the yard gate,
opens it, wanders forward

breaks off one leaf of spotted laurel that's different, almost distorted,
rubs her finger along a central crease that bends it
up like a gondola, shreds it, searches for an insect;

picks one white fruit from a wild strawberry. It's hard,
apparently unripe. She spots a large pebble – rounded as if
it's been in water. There's no river here.

She carries it to paving, throws it down so hard it splits,
gazes a long time at an interior where blue, red,
yellow, green mingle without pattern.

She strokes this surface, traces the lines of swirls
in colours that have been hidden till now
under a pitted exterior.

V for victory

They sit in sun, their backs
to a frosty garden, the room
barely heated. It's wartime

and a jumper's falling apart,
stitches collapsing onto a skein
the old woman's winding.

Sometimes things stick,
there's a tangle of split yarn,
the child tugs,

her grandmother looks up,
Gently, gently,
and sometimes

a frayed length breaks,
small nails scratch
for a new start in matted fabric.

Later the girl holds her hands
upright like spindles, dips and rotates them
weaving liquid, magical circles

while she watches wrinkled fingers,
V-shaped on top of a fattening ball,
hold it steady

while the other hand winds yarn over them
so that it goes on loosely
and a spring survives in tired wool.

The loft

If I'd cared to look I'd have found a hay-chute,
could have imagined hooves on a brick floor.
They weren't real, compared to a door-less doorway
with a sheer drop onto gravel and concrete
approached across crumbly floorboards and holes
that a ten-year old with just enough sense
to look for what was solid, tip-toed round,
putting feet where beams ran underneath
aiming to stand and look down
with the dark depths of the windowless room
a place I could dodge back into. I shinned up
a ladder fixed upright against the wall
which had to be a mast – so the doorway
stood in for a masthead where a cabin boy
became someone everyone looked up to
and able to appear and disappear at will.

Not an egg

A curved lump of stone
that lay where a hen had been scratching
had looked nothing

till my toe knocked it and I saw it
was lined with shapes that looked to me, aged eight,
like four-sided milk teeth in a half open mouth,
their surface a hardness that let me see through
to the same substance thickened and milky, shining back.

I held it to my ear. The sea wasn't there.
I poked my finger in, turned it up, spun the stone round,
caught it, looked again at a nest of tiny pyramids
that shone like raw egg-white
tucked inside a form like a broken shell –

and already uncertain about *egg* and *teeth*
needing years yet to come to *nodule* and *crystal*.
wondered, not who dropped it,
but what cave   cliff   hill
had been home to these sharp edges
with their glinting light, what was it?

One of the North Downs

Turf above Eynsford in March sun,
chalk outcrops and a spread of violets
less shy than those in the garden.
They rested like butterflies,
that had flown in from all the world
as they did in *The Cuckoo Clock*
to turn a nightdress into a ball-gown.
At bedtime drops of blood on her knickers,
nothing to do with flowers.

You need to know

'Thought I was barmy,' she said. 'Oh,' I said.
'Don't mind me talking?' she said. 'Of course
not,' I said and kept my book open.
'Wasn't sex,' she said. Fifty minutes, I thought,
to Gloucester. 'Not at my age,' she said.
Never too old, I thought, but her? She could
be right. 'Forget, don't you, what you look like
I mean.' Just you inside, I thought. Always.
'Jim – that's his name, Jim, has married sons –
but – wanting a man ten years younger
for my Dad – Daddy they used to say.
Father was what I wanted. Sounds sort of
grander somehow. Bigger. What d'you think?
'Depends,' I said. 'You see – I wanted him and
it wasn't sex. That's different, innit?'
'Should be,' I said. You need to know, I thought.
'Felt small and he's taller than me, even so –
but then he laid his hand on my shoulder,
everything was all right.' 'Probably was.'
'Except my wanting him for my Dad.' 'What
was wrong with that? You didn't tell him?'
'No, Not a kid, am I? Something like that,
how could you say it?'

Classic

Gaze always tight to herself,
a thin woman watches her coffee,
sharp against the light.

She stands, turns for her coat,
one fluid movement of pale brown wool
over a body slim as a pillar,

the pose of a caryatid without its fullness
outlined against an old-fashioned lace curtain
that veils a market place and women

with shapes easy-going as potatoes, her dress
the colour of a scrubbed tuber, heavy and free to swing
less revealing than fine, sculpted linen.

She sees me watching,
balances her head
comfortably on her spine.

Two bridges

Those on the smooth bank
contemplated the lowest possible arc,
drawn on heavy paper with an AA pencil.

On the rough side they dreamed
of a shadow under alders, a path twisting down,
an arch reflecting greens and blues.

Both sides looked at the river, its rise and fall,
the way it carried down tree trunks
and tore its banks. They stared across,
perceived names emerging from unseen mouths,
accepted them, wore them with angry pride.

Them pen-pushers calculated ten years
to design, cost, put out to contract, construct.
They'd use gritstone, each block sawn to fit,
a mass that would stand against torrents,
a brain-child risen off paper.

Those slobs *couldn't fix on a date even after evenings*
mulling over the ford, its stones, its disappearances,
gentling arches together from old red sandstone
that would weather to unexpected pinks, oranges, purples,
subside slowly to the lines of a basking otter.

Them snobs saw the town band marching the primary school,
the clergy, the Rotary Club, the mayor onto virgin tarmac,
the world flowing in, visitors exclaiming, *Everything here's*
just lovely. These people have worked so hard.
They'd feel at home at last.

Those layabouts *saw a parapet with a balustrade*
broad enough for children to run on, a place
to rest your elbows, watch salmon and sunlight.
If it took centuries to finish, lumps of rock would lie there,
women would sit on them and tell the old stories.

Them upright knew they'd need a mark at mid-point,
litter bins, a good onwards road to take their lorries
quickly past those hovels, on their own side
a signpost pointing to church, school, town hall,
and, sadly, a guard to watch who came.

Those Neanderthal *knew some day they'd do it*
If they could bring themselves to ask
to be allowed to plant the far end on land
that had always been theirs – bad enough
sweating your guts out for bosses who carped.

Everyone agreed – there had been incidents.
Perhaps the river was the best judge,
keeping them always apart.

Greek café

Today at this waterfront table in the breeze under an awning,
the stink of hot stubs.

It's not illegal here. She has every right. I need only
meditate on what it's doing to her lungs, forget

a daily train-ride in carriages so packed I'd stand with my nose
in a stranger's gabardine and overhead all of them smoking,
my breath clogged;

the staff-room door opening and all of them there, leaning back,
sweeping their hands down in great relaxed circles,
breathing out smog;

shops, hallways, waiting rooms, sitting-rooms, kitchens, bathrooms,
gardens even, infested with it, concentrated in fumes
puffed in my face for a joke;

skirtings from which a dead man's nicotine seeped up
to stain white paint time after time; the day a friend
started to pant on gentle slopes.

Today I passed pieces of lamb and goat, spitted above red charcoal
on sea-front braziers, saw smoke curl up the way ancient writers
describe it rising from roast meat, offered to the gods

so they'd grant favourable winds or ease a soul
on its way to the underworld.

They were wearing their own clothes

They were wearing their clothes
when they arrived.

Their eyes weren't our colour.
Their lips were thick, though some

were narrow as thorns.
They spoke in jabbers.

They worked all hours, piled up money.
We caught them gazing at our houses.

They locked in their women. Their men
lounged about drinking, eyeing our girls.

At night they closed their doors and bred
swarms of children. The smell of their food

decided things – we had to
put them somewhere on their own,

never imagined they'd start drinking
the blood of stolen babies. They sang weird songs.

We built a wall round their quarter. Their eyes
pierced holes in it. We heard them

hammering daggers, shifting sacks of gunpowder.
One of them was caught with a gun and still

we were the only ones willing to strip them
and deal with them the way they needed.

Reading the sea

Terns swoop and screech. I half close my book,
watch them trying to drive off a bonxie.
My finger still touches

the name of one of those Orkney heroes,
forcing me to see it
written out there on Scapa Flow,
where saga merges with sea glitter

that place my mother spoke of,
an impenetrable harbour
somewhere far north

whose sunlit waves even then
covered a fleet of German dreadnoughts,
scuttled where forty years later
the *Royal Oak* went down –

and it
was a catch in my mother's breath
A U-boat got in –

Today my finger's stuck
where a sea-raider orders a rival's lungs
to be pulled through his back
to stand up as bloodstained wings.

Purlingham Magna

A summer day, every wall embroidered with
wisteria and *clematis Montana.* Garages
are thatched, cottages pink-washed, I'm
tempted to aim sonnets at rooflines, lifted
by cosmetic surgery that would gobsmack
farmhands who lived there once, wide-eyed
ghosts in a street where I walk now and
grasp how much love's gone into this magic.
Mellow light dreams over flowers, the same blues
and pinks as heart-shaped padlocks in *Our Shop* –
for him to give her or her to give him?
Whichever – there's no way to grip sunshine.
May still goes on roughing things up with wind.

Bradford Royal Infirmary

Nothing to do but watch
figures pass silently, blurred
by light from stone-framed windows
how they vanish
between the block
that holds the drinks machine
and the far wall of the corridor,
then re-appear – an interrupted
stream of shapes, shrunk
by the gloom overhead –
Oranges and lemons
say the bells of Saint Clements –
children, pushing forward
to squeeze quick as they can
under the raised arms of two adults,
a poised guillotine, singing,
I owe you five farthings, not
thinking of debts, only
how to escape.
White stone walls look strict –
When will you pay me
says the bell of Old Bailey?
The grown-ups' arms
swing down and someone's
caught. At random?
Or do they have their favourites?
Here comes a candle to light you to bed
Here comes a chopper to chop off your head.
As children we ended
rolling on the floor, standing up, laughing.

When shove comes to push

She tautens her back to shove
the barrow against the shed door
and heave it open,

a woman who'd once spent hours
tossing rubble into a skip,
loving its clatter

who now
rests and breathes
before leaning down again and lifting

remembers a Norwegian hotel,
fire-doors one after another labelled with four letters,
'S K Y V ' she puzzled out as *shuv* –

and 'wick, in the name of this village
is Viking. Today she's
not living up to that

her efforts closer
to the restrained French
pousser, push.

His mind turned

A hot afternoon in the cloister, a monk awake since 3.00 am,
his hand travelling by habit across vellum,
his mind running back as he wrote *Banbury*
and someone once did – '*Jesus came to Banbury.*'
his mind running away from a crowd waiting in Bethsaida.

Perhaps he was getting old, his boyhood more insistent –
muddy street, low houses, old men looking up from their drinks,
his brothers shouting, his mother at a door, his first day in the
monastery,
telling the Master of Novices he'd looked down the long road
heard a voice, 'Sequere me,' had been proud
he only among all the boys knew what that meant.

Perhaps he was more aware now
of a series of small things:

Horsemen disappearing. Stories they told on their return.
Old men shouting at him when he could do the job better.
A stone floor where he stood and read the first chapter of St. Mark
aloud to the priest. A cell where it came to him on his knees
how that man must have hoped someone would commend
his teaching to the bishop.

The reeve letting on he felt this one was trouble.
The lord's frown then his nod, the look he gave him
while he clapped the abbot on the shoulder.
The priest saying he wished he'd had the chance.
The lord saying he should thank God for this generosity.

In this new place
he learnt to write so well he was chosen
above his better-born Brothers
to spend afternoons
dipping a brush in lapis lazuli and gold.

Magnifying

Settle to Sheffield –
that's far enough, I'll no longer try
to blow my mind by running round,

though I still picture TRAVEL AND SEE, proclaimed
on mini-buses from bush villages , faces staring out
at traffic lights, government buildings

the way I stared at surf-boats, palms, a woman
skinning an orange with a cutlass,
and thought, them and me, new here

and out there, more
mountains, seas, forests, cities, countries, languages, skills –
learn, understand, be amazed by.

Today I want to sit, or kneel, in a small place –
back garden will do – hold a magnifying glass
close to pock marks on stones,

see the hooks in a bee's tongue
how long it is, how the insect thrusts it down
its feet on a petal,

record nothing, sit and look,
and this will be the way
I'll journey into praise.

The cheese sandwich

watched for a week in 1943
curling under glass in the station buffet;

crunchy with sand from Dawlish beach;
on Mull, better described as a midge cemetery;

of soft Italian cheese and devoured at 3.00 pm in Pompeii
when she'd had nothing since breakfast;

in the pub at Nether Stowey, where it had to be toasted
because there was no butter in it:

snatched from her fingers by Tresco chaffinches;
offered to wild ducks after a visit to a Buddhist monastery

but they'd never heard of *compassion to all modes of being*
and flew away;

crumbly Cheshire an expatriate dreamed of;
Somerset Brie with celery in a bistro in Harrogate;

Local Wensleydale and apple in a pub in Scarborough
though the fruit was Canadian Pink Lady;

of home-made brown bread and a choice of mature Cheddar,
blue Stilton, double Gloucester, Ribblesdale goats',

with pickled onions on Sunday evening
in the back room beside the fire.

Adjustments 1972

I lower my bottom onto earth that's mine
for the first time today, grass
and well-grown weeds. I'll sit right here
to have my 'levs'.
                                        The Co-op fire-alarm
starts up, a sudden extinction, like the dark
in Ghana when the generator failed -

study duty on a night like that, walking
outside the classrooms in the warm scent
that breathes from frangipani or milkwood –
looking at girls who for the moment can't study
the Tudors, Macbeth, the growth of a snowdrop.
They're looking at me now, eyes white in the darkness.

The racket drills in, *You remember classes*
who gave you the boiled-sweet look and hummed?
Teenagers trying it on?   Yes – but they knew
their fathers ran this country now,
colonialists had done what they could,
and except for the label, you agreed?

I look at my garden, creosoted fence,
soft yellow walls, blue slate slowly climbing
to a sky-line of pierced red tiles. Today
I'll scrub myself onto floors, wash paint
till it shines up to meet me. When I've finished
Watford grime will be lodged under my nails.

Then I'll wring out my cloths
and hang them on the docks to dry.

Singing the African Sanctus in Yorkshire

A gentle lift of the conductor's hands
brings us to our feet – no longer strangers
who flocked in from all over,
climbed to this high room, milled round,
flapped off raincoats, settled down –
but, suddenly, a choir.

Eight spaced drumbeats - then
he releases us to ride our breath
up and down the wide sky of three octaves.

Plainsong explodes, *Sanctus, sanctus.*
everything's holy: Egyptian wedding flutes,
Acholi cows, a milking song,
Sufis chanting in the Massa mountains,
the long, undulating flight of the call to prayer.

Hosannas thunder –
the basses off on their own –
while the rest of us just about hold on
among rattles, drums, ululating voices

and everything rises into the rafters
like rooks circling at dusk, layers of birds
folding and unfolding over trees and fields,
the council houses, the Creamery,
while a few break from the mass,
wheel off towards the hills,
are gathered back.

Acid

The guide's torch searches the roof
for a crack where rain got in,
a little acid in every drop
dissolves minerals into flowstone –

The pale circle moves
over blue-green bumps and curves that stir
like hips and shoulders in the kind of darkness
where people carve gods.

Her ear follows an underground river
the habitat of blind white fish –
who'd survive by nuzzling rock –
and she's blundered along duckboards

come finally, last in the group
to stand in a dim space
where she listens to *infiltrating groundwater*
gathered into a stream

and knows it's been seeping into her for years,
stripping off all that numb-lipped trying
to say, think, do the right thing —

That's when he snaps off the torch,
says: *be quiet, imagine.*
and she thinks, let the place speak.

Poetry reading in St. Oswald's

A small platform's been placed
in front of the altar. The Bible

lies closed –

He reads, at an easy pace, lines meant
to fly loose as untied shoelaces.

I lean back in a hard pew,
partly follow, partly track out the way

tracery flows out
and is brought in.

She drops
one word

at a time
into silence

stands,
listens.

I fix my eyes on the text
make out resonances

like slow, full rain, notice the East window
splits a tree, gaze out into leaves

whose masses
must relate to hidden branches.

and think, this house
was built for strange words.

Chopsticks

No candles – the place just a café
they'd dropped into after a lecture -
and perhaps it was the awkwardness
of trying to pick up water chestnuts
with implements that kept their right hands
at such an unfamiliar angle to their mouths
that made them look up at the same moment

and she was finding a way into eyes
she'd often seen expand as if their owner
were having a revelation. Now
they were still, focussed on her,
two right hands were stuck in the air,
she was sucking in rays, thinking
she'd read about this, it was happening
and she was fumbling; not that there was
any question this was the right person,
she wasn't actually blinded - more
checked by the fierceness of that shining,
keeping her eyes up, eating the moment.

Waterfalls

According to brochures
more than one waterfall
is highest in the world.

Is the top the edge where water
turns? Or spray thrown up
above it into sunlight?

Is the bottom
the disturbed surface of a pool
or the basic rock?

Why is the best waterfall
always the highest as if surveyed
from underneath by someone
pointing a rod up
rather than the deepest,
gauged by a chain
trying to find something
water can't shift?

The one I remember
made no world claims
and was frozen that day,
except for a few sly bubbles
sliding down ice tunnels,
dripping silently off.

That unthawing
was enough to make us
draw together and stand,
arms almost touching.

Uranium

I've always wanted to handle the world
and everything in it
with tongs
the way researchers handle uranium.

Smiling a lot is tongs.
Doing little jobs is tongs.
Talking about the weather is tongs.
Listening a long time is tongs.

In labs they keep radio-active material
inside a glass box.
The world
is all round the house.

You, my love, brush aside my handling,
walk in, light up the place
and spread,
insidiously make changes.

After the concert

To the left of the driver's head
numbers keep jumping: 9.20, 3.40, 11.05.
Every time I open my eyes they're different. That clock's
keeping time with a flock of other universes,
each only a tick's thickness away.

Your arm's against mine. At least that's firm
though you're nodding off, re-entering maybe
a dream I'm not musical enough to share.
I glanced sideways in the slow movement
and saw distance in your face.

This coach that now stops and starts, stops and starts
will surge ahead on the motorway, carrying us
in harmonised drowsiness, not caring,
so long as we're together, whether we get home tonight,
tomorrow or the day before yesterday.

My next film

A response to Modigliani 'Madame Z'

The head hangs like a snowdrop at the end of a curved neck,
face a heavy oval, surrounded by tight hair, mouth small, lips
gathered, Japanese style.

Z, he says, not X, as if he wants her half known, hides all her body,
hints at strangely sloping shoulders. Like Mother's. He's providing
a lens for my camera.

I'll work from two images: the first - Mother the day I sat opposite
her at a strange table beside a fish-tank. I was so small my feet didn't
touch the ground, the fish were green needles. We finished
breakfast, I asked to get down, darted behind and looked at her
through water. Fish disappeared into a dazzling cloud, going from
me to her and back.

She took my hand, I walked beside her, very good because she was
so big.

Years later she arrived first at The Caprice and chose a table. I picked
her out through a dispersed glow from electric candelabra, like
dusty glass that waiters slid through. I could make out only the
angle of her head. It wasn't height between us that day but distance –
that grew more dense as I came closer.

Did she too feel that barrier? I'll get Jake to do the script, give him
just those images, enough to let a story grow perhaps into a happier
world.

The opening shot – a woman – who is and is not my mother – seated
at the far end of a restaurant, her lips bunched in something less
petulant than a moue, as if she disdains sadness – or would like to
kiss it. To her left fish sewing water.

Who's won?

Every day as it gets light, she comes,
clings, tries to pull me down
with her into the water.

I gave away the sky-blue jellaba she brought from Egypt
and wore about the house, loose and cool on summer mornings.

Her square bowl with rounded edges and dimpled sides, yellow
deeper than primrose, warmer than butter, under watery glaze,
almost as old as her, was cracked. Every October she'd fill it
and plant three blue hyacinths. I threw it
onto a concrete floor, swept up the pieces.

I gave her silver christening mug to her great grand-child,
took her tart pans to the dump, her oblong cake-tins,
her round cake-tins, the big tin for birthdays and Christmas,
offered a charity shop her toasting fork, her embroidered hankies,
her blue cord dress, her green hat; sold her tea-knives.

She still comes every day first thing. We cling
as we never used to. I can't say, *If you were alive*
you'd be a hundred and five, I'd feel you on my shoulders
hanging on, refusing to get off, weighing me down.

I put on the World Service in the night

to keep company with voices
coming in out of the dark
where everything is.

I learnt who
had been blown up in Afghanistan,
lost in the Kalahari, assaulted in Brixton,

but you weren't news
ignoring health warnings, coming late for treatment.
Statistics bulge with people like that. Many of them, like you

come into grandchildren –
and you had more – books that found readers,
and friends

many of whom
may have turned off a set and lain awake
listening.

Going up to the moor

I turn away from mill, millpond, river
that we explored together last year,
climb steeply up through the trees
out into rain. It streams through
my lashes onto my cheeks.
It feels as if I'm crying.
Which I'm not.

Sunlight arrives dubiously.
I find somewhere to sit, gaze
across a river chasm, bite into
brown bread and lettuce, miss
what I'd longed for – cheese
with its creamy comfort, This other taste
is harsh, there's distance in it, a sourness
like loss, these flakes have to be chewed –

it's grated lemon peel. Someone
must have left a bowl in the fridge
and in my rush to get out
I didn't look.

Something was driving me
to go out and walk
where we walked last year, go on past
and come up here –

I hold bitter rind on my tongue,
try out amusement as a sweetener,
finish my sandwich.

Elegy

Go home
shut your eyes   remember the silence
of a day without wind

grey tree trunks shining in heavy air
buttressed then smooth
up to the lowest branches of a black canopy

a path where pink flowers lay browning,
crush them against your face as you did that day
know what petals lose when they fall

count the cries of a fruit-dove,
listen to leaf-shade as it mottles bark
mould as it subsides

part a tangle of five-fingered leaves
spot clinging underneath
knees bent   white eyed   tree-frog

pull your foot back from a sea of ants
each one grips an egg like a rice-grain
the way a dog carries a stick

a screech   black wings with yellow stripes
bills like capsized canoes
sail across

heavy white trumpets   lilies spot-lit by sunlight
I brought some home   their scent
permeated every room

too much   now
the great trees have been felled